LIBRARY TRAINING GUIDES

Series Editor: David Baker
Editorial Assistant: Joan Welsby

Introduction by the Series Editor

This new series of Library Training Guides (LTGs for short) aims to fill the gap left by the demise of the old Training Guidelines published in the 1980s in the wake of the Library Association's work on staff training. The new LTGs develop the original concept of concisely written summaries of the best principles and practice in specific areas of training by experts in the field which give library and information workers a good-quality guide to best practice. Like the original guidelines, the LTGs also include appropriate examples from a variety of library systems as well as further reading and useful contacts.

Though each guide stands in its own right, LTGs form a coherent whole. Acquisition of all LTGs as they are published will result in a comprehensive manual of training and staff development in library and information work.

The guides are aimed at practising librarians and library training officers. They are intended to be comprehensive without being over-detailed; they should give both the novice and the experienced librarian/training officer an overview of what should/could be done in a given situation and in relation to a particular skill/group of library staff/type of library.

David Baker

LIBRARY TRAINING GUIDES

Induction

Julie Parry

Library Association Publishing

© Library Association Publishing Ltd 1993

Published by
Library Association Publishing Ltd
7 Ridgmount Street
London WC1E 7AE

First published 1993

British Library Cataloguing in Publication Data. A catalogue record for this book is available from the British Library.

ISBN 1-85604-078-X

Typeset in 11/12pt Palermo from author's disk by Library Association Publishing Ltd
Printed and made in Great Britain by Amber (Printwork) Ltd, Harpenden, Herts.

Contents

Preface

The aim of this guide is to demonstrate the benefits of adopting a systematic approach to the design and delivery of induction programmes for new staff in library and information services. More specifically, it sets out to explain the reasons for providing staff induction and to examine the particular needs of different categories of people. The content of a typical induction programme is discussed in some detail, with reminders not to forget the basics such as providing a clean desk and making sure that everyone has someone to take them to lunch on their first day. The methods and skills involved in delivering induction are considered in the context of how people learn and suggestions are made for organizing and administering the whole process. Finally, the guide stresses the role of evaluation in developing a dynamic programme that reflects the needs of the organization and the staff who join it.

In scope, the guide is relevant to all levels of new staff in any type of library and information service, including public, academic and special libraries. Most of the content is applicable to fairly small units as well as large, multi-site operations. The intention has been to provide a guide which is comprehensive without being prescriptive. This is not a manual with step-by-step instructions for designing induction programmes. The needs of libraries and individuals are far too diverse for that. Rather, it should be seen as a cumulation of ideas and approaches to be considered and then adopted or not, according to circumstances. The examples at the end of the guide have been selected from actual induction schemes to illustrate how the concepts can be translated into good practice.

Reference has been made to a number of methods and skills that are not examined in depth in this publication. The selective bibliography lists a variety of texts which will enable the interested reader to go more deeply into techniques such as mentoring, evaluating or delivering a presentation. Further information or advice may also be sought from the organizations listed at the end of the guide.

1 The importance of staff induction

Staff induction, or orientation as it is sometimes known, is the process by which an organization helps its employees to settle in to a new job. The purpose is to enable new staff to become effective within the organization both smoothly and swiftly. Induction involves introducing people to their colleagues and their new surroundings as well as providing information and training. A systematic and well-paced induction programme can significantly alleviate the stress that is natural to anyone embarking on a new stage in their career.

1.1 Reasons for induction

There are many sound reasons why staff induction is important but, above all, it provides an early opportunity to establish a positive relationship between employee and employer. First impressions are often the most lasting, so the way in which new or promoted employees are treated by the organization may well have a significant impact upon their attitude and performance for many years to come. If managers and supervisors fail to use this formative stage to promote corporate values the informal grapevine will almost certainly do the job for them. If this is allowed to happen the end result could be a somewhat confused or inaccurate version of the truth, possibly distorted by minority viewpoints.

1.2 Building relationships

Regardless of its size or structure, the quality of any service can be directly affected by the quality of the working relationships enjoyed by those providing it. Bad feelings in the workroom have a tendency to spill over into the public face of the library service. However, good teamwork and mutual support do not necessarily come automatically to everyone but have to be built up and developed. Of course, some people are able to slip effortlessly into new roles and most eventually manage to build sound relationships with their colleagues. However, the problems of learning to work together productively can be considerably alleviated by an induction programme which pays careful attention to the principles of effective team-building. Explanations about communication channels and staff structures may also help new recruits develop a sense of how and where they fit into the organization as a whole.

Existing staff may be apprehensive about the arrival of newcomers and any ensuing changes to their team and established working patterns. The speed with which a new colleague is accepted into a group may be directly linked to the amount of involvement the other members have in the whole recruitment and induction process. A warm welcome is more likely to be extended by the rest of the team if they know exactly what the newcomer will be contributing to their efforts and have had some input into discussions about the qualities needed for the post. On the other hand, a group of people who are already regretting the loss of a popular colleague may be less inclined to accept a replacement, especially if they are unhappy about the change itself and non-committal about the person who has been selected on their behalf.

1.3 Establishing standards

Anyone starting a new job will be keen to succeed but will find it difficult to do so without a clear understanding of what is expected of them. A formal induction programme provides the ideal opportunity for laying down explicit guidelines about the standards that employees are expected to maintain, in matters of conduct as well as achievement. Most new staff will be eager to meet the expectations of their managers and supervisors but peer pressure can be very powerful and may well exert a stronger influence at ground level, particularly if managers are perceived as distant or uninterested. Newcomers will soon adopt accepted norms of behaviour rather than adhering to rules and regulations that seem to lack authority. For instance, it won't take new staff long to abandon an official dress code which states that suits must be worn if everyone else spends most of their time in jeans and jumpers.

1.4 Performance

Left to their own devices most people will eventually learn how to perform their job and may even do so to the highest standards. However, there is always a danger that skills that are simply 'picked up' may prove to be ineffective or even unsafe. Levels of performance that people are expected to achieve should be made clear, although it should also be stressed that it will be some time before anyone is expected to reach their full potential. It should be explained that induction is a time when mistakes can be made without retribution. After all, the most effective learning often stems from making mistakes, understanding what went wrong and trying to put things right.

1.5 Harnessing enthusiasm

Most people starting a new job arrive with varying degrees of nervousness. At the same time, however, any anxiety is usually mingled with a sense of anticipation and readiness to tackle what lies ahead. After all, having survived the rigours of recruitment, the new employee can justifiably feel a sense of achievement in having got this far. It would be a missed opportunity not to capitalize upon such initial feelings of enthusiasm and motivation. The induction programme should therefore aim to reinforce in the new employee the belief that they are indeed the right person for the job. It should also emphasize the most positive aspects of the work and outline any opportunities likely to arise. At the same time, it is important to ensure that the circumstances surrounding the job are depicted realistically. A sure-fire way of demoralizing staff is to hint at promotion prospects or development opportunities that never actually materialize.

1.6 The new employee's contribution

Ideally, induction should not simply be directed at new employees but should seek to involve them in a two-way process. Employers can benefit greatly from the experience and innovative approaches that new staff can bring. However, the right climate has to be fostered from the beginning. It has to be seen that management is receptive to different points of view and that previous experience is valued in practice, not just in principle. Naturally, the new employee will be expected to fit into the existing culture but the organization which adopts an organic approach to change and development can benefit greatly from the stimulation of new ideas from outside.

1.7 Organizational context

Libraries do not exist in a vacuum but have to evolve to meet the needs of their clients or users. It is important that new library employees understand the relationship between the aims of the parent organization or authority and the role of the library in achieving them. All staff need to develop a clear sense of how they, as individuals, have a contribution to make which is both valid and valuable. Without such an understanding it would not be surprising if employees were to put more energy into achieving their own personal goals than those of the parent organization. If an individual cannot identify with this concept from the beginning it will become progressively more difficult for them to see how their efforts are contributing to any wider achievement. The danger of such a tendency is that it could lead to an increasingly inward-looking workforce providing a service which becomes less and less relevant to the organization.

1.8 Continuing development

Rather than being viewed as an isolated series of events, the training that takes place during induction should be viewed as the beginning of an ongoing process of staff development. Again, the induction period is crucial because it is at this stage that expectations are raised and the foundations laid for future development. It is obviously important that induction training must be well planned, managed and delivered if the recipient is going to continue to place a high value on their own personal development. Getting training off to a good start will certainly help to inspire confidence in the employer's ability to sustain a future commitment to staff development.

1.9 Health and safety

Organizations are legally required to take a responsible attitude towards the health and safety of their employees at work. Accordingly, employers must not only take steps to provide a safe working environment but must also ensure that all their employees understand and are able to put into practice any health and safety measures that exist. Accidents and mistakes are more likely to occur during the early days when everything is new and there seems to be so much to learn. Therefore, suitable training must be made available at a very early stage in the induction programme.

1.10 Reducing staff turnover

One of the reasons most frequently cited for providing induction is to help reduce the level of turnover which can result from a failure to integrate new staff effectively. The costs of rapid staff turnover can be high. Apart from the obvious expenditure on advertisements and interview expenses, hidden costs are incurred in staff time spent interviewing and training. It also takes some time before each new recruit becomes fully productive in post. It is unlikely that the lack of a reasonable induction programme in itself will lead to an early resignation. However, the factors which contribute to a swift departure may well have their roots in the very first days spent in the organization. Someone who feels pride in belonging, who performs to a high standard and has a sound relationship with colleagues is either going to remain giving good service or is likely to leave for a positive reason such as promotion. If the job fails to live up to expectations and the person concerned fails to settle in they may decide to leave as soon as the opportunity arises.

2 Preparation

2.1 A systematic approach

As in most things, a systematic approach to induction will have the advantage of ensuring that nothing important is missed out. By following the same steps on each occasion the planning process will become more familiar and gradually take less time. The initial effort that is necessary to get everything right in the early stages can be transferred to modifying and improving as feedback from evaluation begins to be absorbed into the system. Each time the cycle nears completion the programme should be evaluated and any adjustments which seem necessary made before the cycle begins again. The five main steps are as follows:

- Identify needs
- Plan induction
- Deliver induction
- Evaluate programme
- Make adjustments

2.2 Identifying organizational needs

The needs to be satisfied in developing an induction programme relate to those of the organization or service as well as to those of individuals. Therefore, the starting point for developing an induction programme must be an understanding of organizational aims. There may be a mission statement or a long-range plan which sets out what the organization is trying to achieve. At first glance it may seem that strategic documents at this level have little relevance to such a practical exercise as planning an induction programme. However, no organization is going to pour resources into staff development or training without expecting something in return. The most basic return is a workforce that meets expectations because the staff understand what is required of them and possess the knowledge, skills and attitudes to enable them to perform to the highest standards. Specifically, the organization ought to benefit from induction in the following ways:

- by retaining recently recruited or promoted staff for sufficient time for the organization to receive a reasonable return on its investment
- by developing staff who are both willing and able to work towards organizational goals
- by having a workforce which is skilled, effective and productive
- by reducing the number of personnel problems arising from poor integration

2.3 Identifying the needs of staff

Induction should be provided for all staff beginning a new job, whether they are recent recruits, promotions or transfers. Most induction programmes contain elements that are common to all staff, regardless of the level of their appointment. However, different categories of staff, such as managers or trainees, have induction needs which apply only to their type of post and these must be considered when planning induction. Similarly, there are several categories of people, such as school-leavers or those with disabilities, who may require particular attention. Naturally, any individual may fall into more than one of the following categories.

2.3.1 Support staff

The people who provide clerical and administrative support usually form the majority of staff in most library and information services. Those who are completely new to the service are unlikely to arrive with an in-depth understanding of the nature of library work, so it is particularly important for this group to learn the extent to which their efforts contribute to 'the big picture'. Otherwise it is all too easy for the routine and repetitive tasks which normally form the backbone of library work to be undervalued. It is also desirable to use the induction period to encourage discussion about the roles of other staff and the relationships between them. For instance, newcomers without a library background may fail to appreciate fully the nature of the professional skills practised by qualified staff. It is not appropriate to bombard support staff with mission statements or strategic documents. Their needs will be better served by a jargon-free introduction which enables them to learn where they fit in, what is expected of them and how to perform their tasks.

2.3.2 Paraprofessionals

Staff who do not have professional library qualifications but who do have considerable experience and ability are increasingly employed in positions of some responsibility. They may run branch libraries or have control of a special service and will often have been promoted from within the library. It is important not to neglect to provide induction for these staff, but it must be handled sensitively. Anyone who has spent a long time working for the same employer may not see the need for induction if they are moving up into another job in the same place. In this case induction should be planned carefully to avoid wasting time by going over what the individual already knows. Paraprofessionals may feel somewhat isolated from other colleagues, being senior to other non-qualified staff but lacking the professional training of qualified librarians. The induction process should aim to help them feel secure in their new position and help them to establish effective relationships with staff at all levels.

2.3.3 Professionally qualified staff

The needs of qualified staff will vary according to the type of post they are taking up and the extent of their prior experience. Even those with extensive experience elsewhere will need support and time to help them absorb the culture of their new environment. For those who have recently graduated from library school the transition may come as quite a shock. New professionals tend to be highly motivated and often idealistic. They may find themselves being asked to do tasks for which they feel inadequately prepared or which appear to be inappropriate to their standing. The aim of induction for this category of staff must be to ease their passage into the world of the information professional. An additional difficulty may arise from interactions with other members of staff. Long-established support staff can appear dismissive of newcomers who seem to them to be long on learning but short on experience. New recruits need early support in over-coming such attitudes if they are to avoid the equally undesirable extremes of over-confidence or excessive timidity. The induction period may also serve to disclose any areas of professional competence for which further development is felt to be desirable.

2.3.4 Trainees

Many libraries provide training opportunities for a wide range of people. Some trainees may be graduates gaining experience either before or after obtaining a professional qualification. Others may be youngsters on job experience schemes or more mature people undertaking government retraining schemes. A carefully tailored approach to induction will be necessary to meet the individual needs of trainees. Induction for those just starting out on the professional path should be widened to give them the opportunity to discuss their own future and the profession at large. The tone should be positive and encouraging whilst providing realistic information about the job market and the challenges ahead. Trainees working in support staff roles will need a more basic approach, similar to that adopted for salaried support staff. They may also need additional support themselves, particularly if adapting from a radically different environment. The integration of trainees may be facilitated if existing staff have been helped to understand the purpose and role of training schemes and the needs of the people involved in them.

2.3.5 Managers

Staff in management positions may have been promoted from within the organization. There is a danger of assuming that someone who already knows the people and the surroundings has no need of an induction programme. This is an unwise assumption which could lead to the manager failing to settle into the new job. In such circumstances they may be tempted to hold on to familiar tasks and patterns of work rather than developing to face the challenges of the new role. Specific training in management skills may be necessary for people who have been promoted from posts in which a different set of skills was necessary. Basic orientation for senior staff who are completely new to the organization is just as important as it is for support staff. Managers are also human and have as much need as anyone else to know where the fire exits are and where the paper-clips are kept.

2.3.6 Supervisors

To a certain extent, the needs of supervisors are similar to those of managers, although supervisors tend to have closer links with the staff and the work for which they are responsible. Even the most popular people who are promoted to a supervisory position are likely to experience a subtle change in the way they are treated by their former peer group. This is natural but may come as some surprise to the new supervisor. Induction should concentrate on preparing them to cope with the changes which will inevitably result from their new position. Supervisors who are appointed from outside the organization will have to forge totally new relationships with their team. They will have the added difficulty of not necessarily being familiar with the work in which their team is already engaged. Without careful preparation and a tactful approach to team-building, new supervisors may find resentment and lack of cooperation blocking their progress.

2.4 Different categories of people

2.4.1 *Part-time employees*

It is as important to provide induction training for part-time staff as it is for those who work full-time. However, the logistics of providing induction can be problematical, especially for staff whose working hours fall outside normal office hours. In fact, many libraries rely largely on part-time staff to enable them to provide a service during the evenings and at weekends. If it can be avoided, staff should not be expected to attend any training courses in their own time. If essential training has to be conducted outside contracted hours a considerate and understanding approach should be adopted. Any arrangements must be agreeable to both parties as part-time staff may have other important commitments, such as child care. It may be tempting to assume that staff who work part-time have less need of a full induction programme than others. However, they usually include front-line staff who work at issue desks and enquiry points and with whom most library users come into direct contact. It is, therefore, just as important that this category of staff are as highly trained in providing a quality service as those who do so during the rest of the day.

2.4.2 *Returners*

People returning to work after a break may include those who have had family responsibilities or those who have been unemployed. In either case confidence-building will probably form an important part of induction. Most people will find that the skills they learned years ago have become outdated. Technology changes rapidly and libraries now tend to be computer-intensive places. It is often the case that a fear of technology is rooted in lack of confidence rather than lack of ability. A training programme which is carefully paced and delivered sympathetically will go a long way towards overcoming initial worries about using computer systems. For those returning to work it may be desirable for a significant amount of initial training to take place behind the scenes where hesitancy and mistakes will be less obvious to users and colleagues. Particular attention should also be paid to the social aspects of the workplace. The long-term unemployed may feel sensitive about their background and find the informal exchanges that go on during breaks more of a strain than the work itself. It may be helpful to find ways in which to ease the newcomer gently into situations which they might find personally very trying.

2.4.3 *School-leavers*

Whilst still at school, students are increasingly able to gain work experience which may give them a useful insight into the way that businesses and offices are organized and run. However, work experience differs from the real thing in both duration and intensity. School-leavers may find some initial difficulty in adjusting to the requirements of a job that signifies a serious commitment rather than an interesting change from school. Building relationships with others may need special attention. If the majority of staff are much older than the newcomer it may be difficult to establish any common ground upon which to develop positive relationships. On the other hand, if a number of young people find themselves working together they may be tempted to put more effort into socializing with each other than completing the tasks before them. The knack is to harness enthusiasm and put it to good use rather than letting it get out of hand. School-leavers will probably need a comprehensive training programme which focuses on the full range of skills necessary in libraries. It is less likely that they will arrive with a set of transferable skills than someone who has received training in another type of service or business. Nevertheless, in a supportive atmosphere, where even inexperienced staff feel valued, it can be very rewarding to see school-leavers flourish and develop into valued members of the workforce.

2.4.4 *Ethnic minorities*

When providing induction for staff with different cultural, language or religious backgrounds particular attention must be paid to the skills and attitudes of the managers and supervisors who will be providing the training. They must not only be aware of the existence of any equal opportunities policies but be able to put them into practice. Special training may be necessary to ensure that trainers are well equipped to deal with issues relating to equal opportunities. New staff must be given the opportunity to explain any special requirements and efforts made to meet their needs. Other colleagues also need to be aware of any particular arrangements which have been made and why they are necessary. Careful preparation is the key to success. Without it, existing staff may feel confused or resentful about allowances which have been made on religious or cultural grounds. If they recognize in advance why certain arrangements are being made they are more likely to show tolerance towards and genuine interest in newcomers with backgrounds different to their own.

2.4.5 *Staff with disabilities or special medical conditions*

An induction programme for staff with disabilities or medical conditions must address the needs of the individual. It may be necessary to provide special equipment or make arrangements for access but nothing should be done without consulting the person concerned. The emphasis should be on a practical, shared approach to solving any problems. In this way the newcomer is more likely to feel in control and less likely to feel patronized or burdened with well-meaning but inappropriate gestures. People suffering from epilepsy or diabetes may have their condition well under control but it is essential that others are aware of the situation and know how to cope in case of an unexpected fit or loss of consciousness. Induction provides the ideal opportunity to demonstrate to all staff that everyone, regardless of individual circumstances and needs, has the potential to make a significant contribution to the library service.

3 Planning

3.1 Aims and objectives

Having identified the needs that induction is meant to satisfy, the next step is to decide what measures are necessary to meet those needs. Firstly, it is necessary to state the broad aim or purpose of the induction programme. This statement should then be amplified by specific objectives – an exercise which will not only provide concrete measures against which to evaluate progress but will also encourage systematic planning from the outset. Aims and objectives should preferably be included in an official policy statement which is given to all those responsible for induction as a formal reminder of their obligations. A comprehensive policy document would include statements on the following:

- aims and objectives
- who should receive induction
- who should be responsible for planning, delivery and evaluation
- availability of resources
- content, timing and methods
- relationship to other processes, e.g. probation, continuing development

The following is a typical example of a statement concerning the overall aim or purpose of an induction programme:

- the aim of staff induction is to ensure that new staff become smoothly integrated into their working environment and effective in performing their job

A number of objectives will be necessary to cover the full range of activities that make up an induction programme. The following format is typical:

By the end of the induction programme each member of staff will understand:

- the layout of the library and the immediate environment
- the staff structure and their place within it
- how to follow essential personnel and administrative procedures, e.g. arrangements for taking leave
- their responsibilities regarding health and safety
- appropriate library policies and procedures
- the aims of the parent organization and the role of the library within the organization
- how to perform their job

3.2 Content of the programme

The remainder of this chapter details a whole range of information that would be relevant to most employees on starting a new job. However, in each case the level of detail and timing of delivery would vary quite widely according to the nature of the post and the individuals concerned. The challenge is to identify the needs of each person, or group of people, and devise a programme which meets those needs in terms of pace and method as well as content.

3.3 Pre-induction information

Rather than being treated as an isolated event, staff induction should be viewed as part of a process which begins during recruitment and gradually evolves into normal working life. It is generally at the recruitment stage that potential employees first begin to develop their own perceptions of the organization they are hoping to join. To a certain extent judgement will be based on the known reputation of the organization but it will also be coloured by factors such as the quality of written information provided for job applicants and the way in which candidates are treated at interview. As a result, new recruits are bound to have built up certain expectations even before turning up for their first day. To start work with an inaccurate picture of the job or the circumstances surrounding it will inevitably lead to increased stress levels during the settling-in process, as readjustments have to be made. Therefore, it is important to be aware that the foundations of induction are laid well before the actual arrival of the new member of staff.

There is a certain amount of information which it is essential for new entrants to receive before their first day. Basic instructions for arriving at the right place and at the right time are vital in helping the new member of staff feel that they are able to make an unflustered start and a good first impression. This will not be possible if they are unable to park the car, get snapped at by security staff or cannot find the staff entrance to the library. Accordingly, first day reporting instructions should include:

- who to report to
- where to report
- what time to arrive
- which entrance to use
- parking or travel information

Such basic information may be provided by the library or may be sent out by a separate personnel department.

A friendly welcome to the library may also be offered by sending an informal letter which includes the names of immediate colleagues and a mentor if one is to be used. Brief details of a domestic nature may be helpful, perhaps explaining what lunch arrangements will be made for the first day. A late start may be advisable to allow the staff providing the induction to clear any urgent matters first. However, it must be emphasized to the new staff member which arrangements have been made specially for the first day only, in order to avoid misunderstandings at a later stage.

3.4 Domestic arrangements

The stress of entering a new environment may, for some, be exacerbated by concerns about the most basic functions of life. An early reference to the location of lavatories and arrangements for taking breaks should help to allay anxieties that may prevent the individual concentrating fully on other information. Security of personal belongings will be a matter of immediate concern, so arrangements for hanging coats and storing bags safely should be explained. By offering open access to a wide range of people, libraries occasionally suffer from opportunist crime such as office thefts. If this is the case, the situation should be explained honestly but without being alarmist. It is preferable to emphasize the need for taking a responsible attitude towards reducing opportunities for theft than to give the impression that the environment is rife with crime.

Newcomers, particularly the young and inexperienced, may be anxious about the social aspects of refreshment and meal breaks. Naturally, they will be shown the location of any facilities and be told about the length of time officially allowed for breaks. However, having any local conventions explained at an early stage can ease the stress of feeling new and awkward when everyone else seems at ease with each other. Ideally, people should be warned before starting if they are expected to provide their own mug and coffee or whether there are communal arrangements for buying provisions. A tactful comment to the effect that, 'most of us sit wherever there's space but John always sits in that chair' may help to save embarrassment later when the newcomer enters the staff room on their own for the first time and unwittingly sits in 'John's' chair.

If different arrangements have been made for the first day, such as a later start time or coming in through the public entrance, the usual procedures must be made clear at an early stage. This may include which entrance to use and whether any security passes or codes need to be provided. It may also be helpful to discuss transport arrangements. Those driving to work will need to know about car-parking facilities. Cyclists and motor-bike riders will need to know where bikes may be stored and whether changing facilities are available. Any formal or informal lift-sharing schemes should be explained and introductions made to the relevant people.

3.5 Physical environment

Gaining familiarity with the physical surroundings will have to be phased carefully over a period of time. First priority should be given to certain key locations, gradually widening out to include non-library areas, the surrounding locality and other sites if relevant. A tour led by another member of staff is the most common way of explaining the layout of a building, although a self-administered tour using a printed guide or plan is also possible. A tour should amount to much more than trailing round after an experienced member of staff. It is an early opportunity for newcomers to begin to absorb the character of their workplace. Untidy work areas, peeling notices and heaps of yellowing paper are unlikely to convince the new recruit that they have joined a well-ordered, productive environment. Similarly, if the person leading the tour appears bored or disaffected this is bound to have a negative impact. If the tour is over-long or too detailed the person being shown around may become bored or confused.

The most immediate physical environment for most people will be their desk. The arrival of a new colleague should not herald a frantic search for spare furniture and the necessary equipment must be prepared in advance. Emptying out the previous owner's pencil sharpenings and withered elastic bands may usefully fill some slack moments during the first days but the new owner is more likely to be impressed by a clean working area well stocked with basic stationery and supplies.

The layout of the office or workroom should be explained briefly at the start, indicating any particular equipment which will be used regularly. Details about workflows, location of supplies and equipment for occasional use should all be saved for later on in the induction programme. The same principle applies to the library itself and its wider surroundings. Decide which are the most important features and emphasize them without dwelling too long on any one aspect. It may be helpful to relate key areas to each other to help people find their bearings when they are on their own. For example, a newcomer is more likely to remember that the staff photocopier is 'in the office with a blue door, opposite the tea room' than recalling that it is in 'room 4C'.

3.6 Personnel information

Almost invariably, part of the first day will involve a certain amount of form-filling and explanations about various procedures. Some of this may be conducted by personnel staff or it may all be handled by library staff. The approach should be friendly but carefully structured to ensure that no vital information is missed. As a lot of detail is involved it is wise to provide the information in writing, backed up by a verbal explanation with plenty of opportunity for questions. It is worth checking not only that the individual has the necessary official paperwork but that they fully understand the content and significance of everything. This may involve spending some time going over the contract and terms and conditions of service. A discussion about salary and options for payment could include an explanation about payslips, deductions, overtime arrangements and claiming expenses.

At an early stage, information should be provided about what to do in case of sickness or unexpected absence. It may be useful if people are advised to keep a copy of such procedures, including telephone numbers, at home, where they are more likely to be of use in an emergency.

Starting, finishing and break times need to be explained clearly. Those who are new to the work may not be familiar with the shift systems that operate in most libraries and may fail to appreciate why some people seem to have breaks at unusual times. Even those with library experience may find a more rigid or lax regime than they have been used to. It is for their benefit, as well as in the interests of efficiency, that they understand what is and is not acceptable in their new employment. For example, if it is standard practice for latecomers to have to make up the time during the same day, this should be made clear at the outset and preferably in writing. The information should also be realistic rather than idealistic. The rule might state that tea-breaks must last a maximum of 15 minutes but if most staff habitually take 30 minutes the newcomer will soon succumb to peer pressure.

Arrangements for taking annual leave should be explained and any necessary paperwork handed over. Leave cards should be accompanied by instructions about how they should be filled in and authorized. Any time away from work, including time in lieu and flexitime, may be subject to certain restrictions and these must be made clear. For instance, in academic libraries it may not be possible to take annual leave during term time. Again, these matters should ideally be covered on the first day and backed up with written information to guard against any later misunderstandings.

It is appropriate to mention the arrangements for union membership at this stage, although a formal approach by a union official will probably take place later on. Most people appreciate knowing what options will be open to them, even if the procedures actually take place on some future occasion.

During induction, the new member of staff must be made aware of any appraisal scheme or measures relating to pay. It is also helpful to refer to the existence of disciplinary and grievance procedures, although without going into unnecessary detail. It is likely that the new employee will have to undergo a probationary period and the process should be explained carefully, including information about what will happen if progress is unsatisfactory during this period.

3.7　Health and safety

The basics of health and safety should certainly be covered during the first week at work, although preferably not during the first day. A tour will be necessary to point out the location of fire exits, fire extinguishers and other emergency equipment. A practical exercise in which fire extinguishers are actually discharged can be a lively way of ensuring that staff really know how to operate them but, obviously, this type of training should only be attempted under expert supervision. The extent to which each individual is expected to take responsibility for health and safety issues must be explained clearly. Supervisors cannot watch everyone all the time so employees need to understand their own safety obligations when lifting heavy weights, climbing ladders or pushing loaded trolleys.

In automated environments all staff should be alerted to the need for a sensible approach to VDU work and the necessity for taking regular breaks to rest the eyes. Getting the ergonomics of the workplace right can help prevent all manner of problems, from eyestrain to backache. However, not everyone is aware of the extent to which they can and should make adjustments to improve their immediate working environment. It may be necessary to provide practical guidance on achieving a comfortable position for an adjustable seat or the optimum angle for a light.

Personal safety is a major issue in many libraries these days. Again, the new recruit needs to be given a frank account of any potential dangers and the safeguards that exist. It is sensible to provide a formal and accurate assessment of the risks to forestall any lurid anecdotes that might find their way along the informal grapevine. It is important to ensure that all new staff know the location of, and are able to operate, any security alarms, panic buttons or other communication devices.

3.8　Introductions

In a smaller library introducing a new member of staff does not pose a great problem. However, in larger libraries with numerous staff it can be very confusing for the new recruit to meet too many people at once. Nevertheless, it is natural for existing staff to be curious about new colleagues and eager to meet them. A reasonable approach in these circumstances is to let everyone know in advance who is going to start work and when, and tell them to expect to be introduced at some point during the first week. This enables new recruits to meet first with their direct supervisor, members of their immediate team and their mentor, if used. Meetings with other members of library staff and senior management can then be spread out over the first week. Senior members of staff will need to meet a variety of non-library employees. While it may be reasonable to expect such people to establish their own contacts it is helpful if a few key appointments are arranged before the newcomer takes up post.

3.9   Introduction to the organization

It is surprisingly easy for staff to become so entrenched in the daily routine that they lose sight of what their parent organization is engaged in trying to achieve. Employees can hardly be expected to demonstrate a high level of commitment if they have never identified with the aims of the authority, institution or company for which they work. Certain commercial companies offer a lead in this respect as they place a lot of emphasis on fostering pride in the corporation. Feeling good about belonging forms a vital element in the orientation of new employees in such organizations.

The present circumstances of the organization are bound to be of interest to someone who has just joined it. For example, is the institution undergoing expansion or contraction or are there mergers in the offing? Obviously new employees will want to be advised if there are any potential threats or opportunities which may directly affect their jobs. Again, the timing and presentation of such information will depend on individual circumstances. Senior managers will need to know at the earliest stage but to new library assistants it may be of less immediate concern.

3.10   The library within the organization

As well as understanding the purpose of the parent organization, it is also important to recognize the role of the library in achieving corporate aims. In order to develop a grasp of the issues senior staff will need to be furnished with copies of mission statements, strategic plans and other documents. Staff at other levels should not be overburdened with paperwork but are still more likely to feel a sense of achievement if they can see the extent to which their own efforts and those of their team contribute to much wider goals. Library work inevitably involves many routine tasks. The individual who not only sees the necessity for those tasks but also understands how they contribute to the success of the organization is much more likely to feel fulfilled at work. The foundations of understanding these concepts are laid down during the induction process.

In order to engender a sense of belonging new employees need to know how they fit into the scheme of things. A well-produced and accurate staffing chart can provide a clear picture of the relationships between different staff members. On the other hand, an inaccurate, out-of-date chart is worse than nothing and is unlikely to inspire any confidence at all in library management. Communication structures should certainly be explained so that the new recruit knows exactly who their supervisor is, who they are responsible for and who should be consulted about what. The newcomer may be interested to hear about newsletters and other forms of communication. Later on it will be appropriate to describe the meetings structure and indicate what opportunities may be available for attending meetings and participating in working groups.

The nature of relationships with other sections or departments may have a bearing on the way the library's business is conducted. For example, in academic libraries it may be the case that some library staff are employed on academic contracts and spend substantial amounts of time out of the library attending faculty meetings and teaching. To the new recruit it may appear that such staff are neglecting their duties in the library. This could result in resentment and ill feeling unless it is clearly understood by everybody that academic library staff are, in fact, actively engaged in promoting the library service to the wider academic community.

3.11 Policies, standards and expectations

A new recruit will be anxious to succeed and will want to fit smoothly into the organizational culture. The organization will want this too and most will have certain standards to which all staff are expected to conform. Whilst it may be left to chance, and people may well pick up acceptable behaviour from colleagues, it is far better to be systematic in explaining what the expectations are. In the early stages it is best to explain the most basic policies and point out that actual training in putting them into practice will take place at a later date. Further training may then be provided in whatever skills are necessary, such as telephone manner, handling difficult customers or interpersonal skills. Certain policies, such as equal opportunities or rules on smoking, should be brought to the attention of new staff at an early stage.

3.12 Learning the job

Many people will be anxious to get going on their new duties but the first day will normally be fairly full with other essential matters. Providing an induction timetable will reassure the new employee that starting to learn the job does feature among all the other items to be covered. Before becoming involved in the job itself it is worth the supervisor spending some time going over the job description and recapping exactly what the post involves in order to avoid any misconceptions. A useful technique for staff whose work will be of a reasonably routine nature is to provide an outline of the typical working day. This method enables staff to gain some sense of security from understanding how their work will be structured.

Ideally, the programme should aim for a smooth transition from initial arrival when very little actual work is done to the end of the induction period when the individual has completely settled in and begun to become effective in post. However, many people like to feel that they are achieving something concrete right from the start, so they should be able to get on with a straightforward task from a reasonably early stage. The key is to ensure that the person understands why they are doing that task, how to do it and who to ask in case of difficulty. It is helpful to start with something basic which can be picked up relatively quickly and returned to as necessary. Throughout the induction period more and more tasks and responsibilities will be added.

3.13 Continuing development

It has already been stressed that induction is not a stand-alone process but serves to provide a bridge between recruitment and continuing development. Accordingly, the opportunity should be taken during induction to discuss continuing development and approaches to training. The new recruit will need to know how training needs are assessed and the extent to which they will be expected to take responsibility for their own development. They will need to get a feel for whether the organization fosters a culture of development or whether opportunities are going to be limited by financial constraints or lack of commitment by senior management. Procedures should be explained for applying for funding or time off for attending courses or other events. It may be useful to refer briefly to the type of opportunities of which others may have taken advantage in the past. Everyone needs to know which forms to fill in, where they are kept, who needs to authorize training and what is expected in return, such as a formal report or an evaluation form.

Organizational attitudes to external professional commitment and membership of professional bodies should be made explicit. Some organizations may actively encourage such involvement while others leave it entirely to the individual. Whatever the situation, a close match between expectations on both sides will make for a more productive relationship.

3.14 Employee benefits

A fairly obvious way of making the new employee feel good about their new situation is to spend some time discussing the benefits to which they are entitled. These may range from financial benefits to social and recreational opportunities. If information about pensions has not been provided as part of the discussion about pay and conditions of service the available options could be mentioned at this point. Other financial benefits could include luncheon vouchers, subsidized meals or cheap rates at sports centres. Many larger organizations have clubs or staff associations which organize regular events and meetings. Library staff themselves may arrange group outings and social events. The newcomer should be made aware of any such arrangements and invited to join in as appropriate.

4 Delivery

4.1 Delivering induction

The way in which induction training is delivered should receive as much attention as the content. The aim should be to present the programme in a stimulating manner which facilitates learning. The most carefully conceived induction course will lose much of its impact if those responsible for delivering it are lacking in expertise or commitment. It is vital that everyone involved in contributing to the delivery of induction understands the purpose of what they are doing and, if necessary, receives appropriate training themselves. Working examples of induction programmes and courses are provided at the end of this guide.

4.1.1 *Timing*

Timing is a critical factor in the success or failure of an induction programme. Not only does the overall duration need to be considered, but also the pace of delivery. There is no special formula for getting the timing right for everyone, as individuals learn and develop at different speeds. For this reason it is important to build in regular checks on progress in case the pace is proving too fast or too slow. Similarly, some flexibility should be built in to enable the programme to be modified if unforeseen circumstances prevent it from running exactly as planned.

It is generally agreed that too much information in the early stages can lead to new recruits becoming overloaded and unable to absorb anything further. At the same time, if there are too many unfilled hours in the early days people will become bored and generally start to feel dissatisfied by their apparent lack of progress. The combination of having to learn new skills, acquire knowledge and take on new responsibilities can initially seem very daunting. For this reason, it often helps to break down a large job into a number of smaller, more readily achievable tasks. Similarly, successful induction programmes are often divided into sections covering the first day, the first week, the first month and so on. This structure can be seen clearly in some of the sample checklists. Obviously, the most important aspects must be covered first and these will generally involve personnel information and domestic arrangements. Other information can be phased in over a period of time. Ideally, as a new member of staff gradually settles in, the induction process will give way to full productivity. However, the whole undertaking may last for some time, possibly up to several months for senior professionally qualified staff. As it may seem dispiriting if the programme seems to rumble along indefinitely without an obvious structure, the provision of clearly defined, attainable goals is desirable.

4.1.2   *The learning environment*

New staff are likely to gain most from an induction programme which is delivered in conditions which are conducive to learning. The term 'learning environment' may refer to the physical surroundings in which training takes place or it may also describe the less concrete, but equally important, matter of corporate attitude to staff development. If the organizational climate is supportive of development it should be a relatively straightforward matter to manage induction as a single component of a much larger portfolio of staff training activities. Existing expertise in planning, implementing and evaluating staff development can readily be transferred to the induction process. In an organization where opportunities and funding for training are limited, induction may be the only form of staff development which can be provided for everyone without involving expensive courses or external trainers.

The physical environment may also help or hinder effective learning. For an induction course that is held away from the workplace the normal rules for running training events should apply. This means paying attention to factors such as heating, lighting, room layout and ensuring that the course is not subject to unnecessary interruptions. Obviously, induction that is more directly job related and takes place in the normal work environment will be subject to the same pressures as the job itself. However, it is helpful if the induction period can provide a certain amount of 'protection', perhaps by re-routeing telephone calls or asking others not to dump large piles of paperwork on the newcomer's desk.

It may be helpful to all concerned if some indication can be given when training is taking place. Library users will assume that the person behind the desk is well equipped to deal with their requirements efficiently and accurately. They may react badly if the service is particularly slow or the librarian seems to be unable to cope with a fairly simple transaction. Not all job training can be conducted behind the scenes, so when it comes to dealing with users face to face for the first time it is worth acknowledging that slight delays are possible. New staff may be offered the option of wearing a 'trainee' badge or a discreet notice can be used to explain that training is taking place, asking customers to be patient. Most people are reasonably understanding as long as they are aware that someone is learning the job. Equally, the colleagues of new staff are more likely to be tolerant of slowness or lack of knowledge if they are fully aware that training is taking place. Empathy will be even greater if all staff regularly undertake their own staff development activities and are able to relate the progress of others to their own learning experiences.

4.1.3   *How people learn*

One of the major reasons why people fail to learn is because they are not motivated to do so. Fortunately, at the start of a new job most people feel positively motivated and willing to learn. However, motivation may soon be lost if staff are unhappy or sense that they are failing to progress. Research has demonstrated that individuals have different approaches to learning and this factor must be taken into account when designing an induction programme. Whilst some people prefer to jump right in and try things out for themselves others may be somewhat tentative and prefer a more measured approach. It is hardly practicable to conduct assessments at the beginning of employment in order to tailor a programme to the learning needs of individuals. Therefore, the delivery of the induction programme must be designed to offer a wide variety of approaches to meet the different learning styles of the people concerned.

It is generally accepted that strategies which are 'learner-centred' are most likely to result in the effective acquisition of new skills and knowledge. This does not mean abandoning newcomers to find out everything for themselves. It means enabling them to become more involved in their own learning and to take a degree of control over the process. Information which has to be actively sought, perhaps in a fact-finding exercise, is more likely to be retained than that which is delivered in a lecture. Similarly, skills have to be rehearsed, possibly many times, until the individual feels comfortable about putting them into practice. Focusing on the needs of the learners offers them the opportunity to have some input into the decision about when they are ready to undertake a task on their own. To timetable a session in which staff are *taught* a skill may not necessarily result in everyone *learning* the skill to the required standard. Therefore, an induction programme should take account of this and build in enough flexibility to allow for the varying amounts of practice and feedback that different individuals may require.

Adequate levels of support are essential to the success of learner-centred methods. New staff need to know who is responsible for all aspects of their training and to feel able to ask for help when they need it. Trainers and mentors need to be sympathetic to the difficulties experienced by learners. By having access to supportive members of staff and by having some control over their own development most people will feel motivated to learn and will react in a positive manner to their new working environment.

4.1.4 Learning objectives

As already indicated, aims and objectives must be established to ensure that the induction programme itself develops in a controlled and systematic manner. In addition, specific objectives or learning outcomes should be formulated for each section of the programme. By working towards these, new recruits are more likely to gain a sense of purpose and an awareness of how well they are progressing. Objectives or learning outcomes should be carefully phrased to state what knowledge or skills will have been acquired by the end of an exercise. For example, a set of practical learning objectives for an issue desk training session could follow this pattern:

By the end of the first session participants will be able to:

- use the computer to issue and check in standard loan items
- use the book-check unit to sensitize and desensitize items
- make correct use of bar-code reader and date stamp

The objectives of a session designed to impart information about the interlibrary loans system could be worded as follows:

By the end of the session participants will understand:

- the role of national and regional lending schemes
- the automated interlibrary loans system
- the work of the interlibrary loans team

In both examples the emphasis is on what the participants are expected to learn and, as long as the objectives are met, demonstrable skills and knowledge should result. If the objectives merely state that 'staff will be shown how to issue books' or that 'the interlibrary loans system will be explained' there is no guarantee that the necessary skills or knowledge will actually be acquired. Meaningful evaluation of the whole process is largely dependent upon the nature of the objectives set.

4.1.5   *Induction courses*

In a large library service where new staff are appointed on a fairly regular basis it may be possible to devise a standard induction course to cover elements which are common to everyone. Many large organizations run such courses for all their recruits and library staff may find themselves joining colleagues from widely differing backgrounds. In such a case the library will have little or no say in the structure, timing or content of the course but it is worth taking advantage of the opportunity and combining it with other, more library-oriented induction. Despite certain limitations there are a number of benefits to be gained from offering a standard programme:

- it is cost effective to provide induction for several staff at once
- those providing induction can build up expertise
- a sense of belonging to the wider organization may be engendered
- staff are given the opportunity to establish relationships outside their immediate team

The way in which a course is structured can vary widely. It may be short and intensive, covering no more than two or three days, or it may take place over a much longer period, interspersed with other forms of training and job familiarization. It may consist of a number of free-standing modules which may be run or attended as the need arises. However, no matter how comprehensive a course, it should be supplemented by an approach which takes account of individual needs.

4.1.6   *Individual programmes*

An individual approach will certainly be necessary in smaller organizations and in those where staff turnover is relatively low. In addition, there are certain aspects of induction which simply do not lend themselves to mass training. For example, the importance of building effective relationships has already been stressed but this has to take place between the individuals and their teams. It cannot be achieved by attending a course, although the principles of team-building may certainly be covered in a more general context. Job familiarization also features in the induction process but most new staff will be undertaking different responsibilities for which a more individual approach is more appropriate.

4.2   Methods

There are many teaching and learning techniques which can be adopted for delivering an induction programme which suits both the resources of the library and the needs of its new recruits. It is worth considering a number of different techniques in order to accommodate a range of learning styles. Certainly, variety is likely to make for a more lively and stimulating

programme. Some of the following methods will be most relevant to group induction whilst others are more suited to an individual approach.

4.2.1 Tours/visits

One of the key aims of induction is to enable new staff to become familiar with their surroundings. Maps and plans are very useful but should not be used as a substitute for seeing the real thing. The importance of using an experienced member of staff who will make the tour interesting and relevant was stressed in Section 3.5. This method has the advantage of allowing informal introductions to take place at the same time, although care must be taken not to overwhelm the individual with too many new faces. If a person's mentor is also their guide they can use a tour as an opportunity to begin to get to know each other.

A more learner-centred approach may be adopted by setting new staff the task of finding various locations themselves. This method requires careful initial preparation and a feedback session afterwards so it is not simply a quick and easy way out of organizing a tour. It is, however, particularly suitable if several new staff join at the same time. Working in pairs or small groups is ideal and a list of places or things to be found should be provided, together with clear guidelines about timing and what to do in case of getting lost. There is no reason why the learning should not also be fun but care must be taken not to seem patronizing. Some people might find the idea of a treasure hunt lively and stimulating but others could view it as a rather undignified introduction to their new employment.

Organized visits accompanied by an experienced member of staff are a more appropriate way of showing people different departments or distant sites. The guide or group leader can then take responsibility for introductions to managers and for transport arrangements if necessary. Again, careful preparation is vital. It is unreasonable for anyone to turn up in another department, without advance warning, and expect someone to find the time to explain the work of their section. Those attending the visit need to know beforehand where they are going and what to expect, the times of departure and return and what to do about meals or claiming expenses. Special arrangements may have to be made for part-time staff whose working hours would not normally coincide with the visit period.

4.2.2 Lectures/presentations/talks

A tried and tested method of imparting information to a group is to stand up and talk to them, with or without the use of audiovisual aids. It is certainly a cost-effective way of presenting a significant amount of factual material to large numbers of people. Unfortunately, not everyone who delivers a lecture has the ability to hold the attention of their audience and deliver a message which remains with the listener. In fact, the actual learning that results from attending a lecture is often more limited than in a situation where participation is greater. Nevertheless, there are circumstances where a talk is the most appropriate solution. For example, senior managers may use the technique to present the public face of the organization, or colleagues may devise presentations to explain the nature of their jobs. It should be remembered that it is natural for an audience to lose concentration as time progresses, so sessions should preferably be limited to 30 minutes or 45 minutes at the most, allowing extra time for questions.

4.2.3   *Group learning*

Various techniques may be employed with smaller groups to provide a more participative experience. Working with others in a seminar group can provide a useful introduction to problem-solving within a team. Case studies and role play can be highly effective ways of replicating real-life situations in a protected environment. Situations requiring interpersonal skills, such as customer care and assertiveness, are well suited to small-group learning. However, these types of training should be conducted only by skilled and experienced personnel as in the hands of incompetent trainers the results may be ineffective or even potentially harmful.

4.2.4   *One-to-one training*

Training on a one-to-one basis involves an experienced person teaching the newcomer the skills necessary to carry out a task. The success of learning by 'sitting next to Nellie', as it is often disparagingly called, depends largely on the ability of the trainer. A competent trainer must understand the principles of effective learning, be able to communicate clearly, know how to offer praise or constructive criticism and be able to spot potential problems. It is important to ensure that correct procedures are taught and that bad habits which may have crept into common practice are not passed on. It is true that this is a labour-intensive form of training but the opportunity for constant interaction and feedback between those involved makes it a productive method. Initial training may take place off the job by setting up simulated exercises. When the new recruit feels confident, training can take place on the job with the trainer on hand until both feel that the trainee is ready to work alone.

4.2.5   *Self-directed learning*

There is a place in induction for a certain amount of self-directed learning. Induction programmes can involve a lot of interactive learning so it is useful to intersperse other activities with a slowing of pace to allow for reflection and consolidation. Flexibility at this stage will enable individuals to concentrate on any aspect they are finding personally challenging. Time should be allowed for reading as most people will have at least some paperwork to tackle, whether it be instruction manuals or policy statements. Any form of self-directed learning must be conducted within a supportive environment with someone available to answer questions, if necessary. It must be made clear that self-directed activities are as important as any other part of induction and should not be presented simply as an opportunity to take things easy for a while.

4.3   Supporting material

All of the methods outlined above can be made much more effective by the imaginative use of supporting material. While care and attention is important in presentation it is not essential to have access to sophisticated production methods, such as desk-top publishing. As long as they complement the organizational style, simple hand-outs executed with care can be just as effective as glossy brochures. A tape/slide presentation may be less sophisticated than a video but may make no less impact as long as it is well produced. Very often the most simple solutions are the most elegant.

4.3.1 Audiovisual aids/video

A number of audiovisual options can be used to enliven presentations. Using an overhead projector is a standard method of stressing key points. Slides or tape/slide packages may also be used to provide visual stimulation. The quality of such material can have a major impact on the overall standard of the presentation. A competent performance may be perceived as poor if it is accompanied by transparencies which are illegible or inappropriate to the subject whereas the same performance may be considerably enhanced by the use of lively, pertinent images. However, even the most stimulating audiovisual aids cannot compensate for a presentation which is inherently dull in delivery and irrelevant in content.

Some larger organizations may produce their own promotional or training videos which can help to provide variety during an induction programme. Commercial videos may be very expensive but have the advantage of being professionally produced to a very high standard. They are generally geared more towards continuing staff development than induction but they may also provide a stimulating introduction to topics such as customer care, time management or health and safety.

4.3.2 Printed materials

There is no escaping the need for written material during induction. Because such a lot of information is provided it is essential to reinforce other methods of delivery with a comprehensive range of documentation. This gives new staff the opportunity to check, at their own pace, their understanding of what they have been told. Much of this material will be referred to quite heavily in the early days and some may be retained for use well into the future. It goes without saying that the content must be accurate and written in clear, jargon-free language. The aim should be to produce material which is up-to-date and relevant in content, reflecting the kind of image that the library wishes to promote.

Leaflets and information produced for library users can give new staff an insight into the range of services offered. Such material is very suitable for new staff as there should be no expectation that the reader has any prior knowledge or understanding of the library's internal workings. They also provide further evidence of how the library sees itself. A dynamic, professional service is likely to portray itself as such in its promotional literature. On the other hand, a set of uninspiring and poorly reproduced documents may well reinforce the impression that the service itself is staid and lacks dynamism.

Staff handbooks are an important form of communication. They can provide official information about all aspects of the library service and also about the parent organization. They often contain staffing and structural charts which are valuable because most people appreciate seeing not only where they fit into the library structure but how the library fits in to the authority or institution as a whole. Matching names to posts makes for more interesting reading but the disadvantage of including names is the speed with which they change and the necessity for frequent updates. Committee structures, lines of responsibility and decision-making processes will be of particular interest to managers and other senior staff.

Instruction manuals and guidelines can cover a range of topics from health and safety procedures to how to answer the telephone. The format may vary from large, comprehensive folders to individual hand-outs. The new recruit will certainly need to have access to this type of information but should not be swamped with vast amounts of paperwork in the early stages. A useful compromise is to make sure that people are aware of the existence of staff manuals and operational guidelines but are provided with their own copies of key documents only, possibly extracted from the more complete versions. Again, the best approach is to hand over a manageable amount of material which is well produced, lucid and relevant to the needs of the individual.

4.4   Induction providers

A number of different people will generally be involved in providing induction and each will have a different contribution to make. Careful consideration should be given to the selection of staff to provide the training, as those who are competent at their own jobs may not necessarily make the best trainers. It is essential that all those involved have a clear understanding of their responsibilities and feel confident about the training they are expected to carry out. They must know how to spot when things are going wrong and what to do in case of problems. Ideally, anyone in this position should themselves have undertaken training in how to deliver training.

4.4.1   *Supervisors*

Supervisors play a key role in the induction of new staff. Ideally, they should have been involved in the recruitment process as well as in the development of the induction programme, in which case they will bring a useful amount of background knowledge to the exercise. If this has not happened, they must be briefed in advance. Supervisors need to be fully aware of their responsibilities regarding new staff. They must know exactly what training they are expected to conduct themselves and how to ensure that any other necessary training does take place. They need to be aware of their responsibility for establishing and maintaining standards. They certainly need to know how to spot problems and to whom difficulties should be referred if they are unable to resolve them. They also need to develop and maintain motivation in their staff as well as understanding the value of providing regular feedback and offering praise when due. As the person with whom a new recruit will have the most contact, it is essential that the supervisor is able to establish a relationship based on trust and respect.

4.4.2   *Mentors*

It is increasingly common practice to assign new staff with a mentor, sometimes known as a sponsor or 'starter's friend', who will act as a friend and adviser to the new recruit. The role of a mentor is essentially supportive and care must be exercised in selecting a person who will relate well to the newcomer. Peers, particularly those who have recent experience of being new themselves, often make excellent mentors. Supervisors or others with managerial responsibility are not suitable as the aim is to provide informal support to augment the formal system. Initial lack of confidence and feelings of being overwhelmed are not uncommon and a good mentor will be able to help put things into perspective. At the same time they must keep alert to the possibility of fundamental and serious problems which should be referred to supervisors or managers. Sound communication skills are essential and listening skills are particularly important. A mentor is the ideal person to conduct an initial tour of the building and to carry out informal introductions. Normally, they will have a high profile at the beginning of induction but their involvement will gradually decrease as the newcomer settles in and begins to establish other relationships. However, in some organizations, mentoring is a long-term commitment which supports the development of staff throughout their career.

Mentors must be adequately prepared for their role. It is not enough to assign someone to take responsibility for a newcomer and then simply leave them to get on with it. It must also be made clear that, although they are being asked to take responsibility for the initial well-being of a new colleague, there is no compulsion to establish a lasting friendship.

4.4.3   *Colleagues*

A number of other people will inevitably be involved in the induction process. Learning new tasks will often be achieved by one-to-one training and this may be conducted by work colleagues, although the supervisor will usually be responsible for overseeing the process. Obviously, the person training needs to know how to carry out the task properly and have sufficient background knowledge to be able to answer questions and put the job into context. Also, they must be able to demonstrate good practice and explain how the task should be performed. Patience, tact and a flair for communication are essential qualities for anyone engaged in passing on skills to their colleagues.

4.4.4   *Managers*

Managers have a vital role to play in communicating the ethos of the service. Many staff will not have regular contact with senior management, so a special effort should be made during induction if managers are not to be perceived as distant beings who have little interest in their staff. Brief introductions should certainly be carried out during the early days and there may be a variety of ways in which managers can be involved in the programme. For example, they could contribute presentations to a formal course, or lead seminar and discussion groups.

4.4.5   *Non-library staff*

Most organizations have personnel or human resources departments whose staff will have varying degrees of involvement with the library. They will almost certainly have taken a leading role in recruitment and may have a significant input into induction, either at a policy-making level or at a practical level by running induction courses. They may also be able to provide valuable quantitative and qualitative information from exercises such as ethnic monitoring and exit interviews. Other staff who could have a role in induction include union representatives and specialists from other services such as computing or finance.

The library should make particular efforts to ensure that all staff who are involved in induction, from whichever section or department, are fully aware of the role of the library within the organization, what it is trying to achieve and the particular needs of those who work within it. The library needs to ensure that its voice is heard because the way in which staff are treated outside the library may well have implications for their general attitude within it.

5 Organization and evaluation

5.1 Organizing induction

As there are many strands to induction a systematic approach to its organization and administration will help to ensure that nothing important is overlooked. Although many different people may be involved, overall responsibility for managing resources, maintaining standards and the ongoing development of the programme should ideally rest with one person. Much of the implementation may be delegated to others but the induction manager must ensure that everyone involved has a clear understanding of the range and nature of their responsibilities.

5.1.1 *Record-keeping*

Statistical and non-statistical data should be collected and analysed regularly to monitor the induction activities being undertaken. Such information not only enables the induction manager to keep track of the whole process but aids evaluation and may prove invaluable when bidding for resources. As a minimum, the following records should be kept:

- names of new staff, trainers and mentors
- statistics relating to staff turnover
- financial records
- copies of induction courses and programmes
- feedback records

It is worth retaining copies of all induction programmes and courses to help in developing improved versions. A formal record of training may also prove useful if there are concerns about an individual's performance, particularly during the probationary period. Obviously, confidentiality must be respected; if personal records are held they must always be kept locked away.

5.1.2 *Checklists*

A suitable method must be chosen for assembling all the different elements of induction into a coherent package. A tried and tested technique is to produce checklists which enable staff to see at a glance what has or has not been done. A number of examples are provided at the end of this guide. The design can vary, sometimes taking the form of tabulated sheets requiring signatures and countersignatures. Other checklists provide boxes to be ticked on completion and some simply list what needs to be done. Any of these options is acceptable although it is worth remembering that many people like the sense of achievement to be gained from literally checking things off as they are completed.

If checklists are used they should be presented as an essential part of the process and the importance of completing all sections must be stressed. They should be used during review meetings to check progress and any sessions which have been missed should be rescheduled. The reviewer or supervisor should perhaps be wary if a new recruit completes their induction period with a pristine checklist bearing a row of ticks which all look as if they were made at the same time with the same pen. A dog-eared document full of scribbled notes may look less appealing but its owner could well have been more conscientious about carrying it around and undertaking everything they were scheduled to do.

Checklists are useful not only for new recruits but also as an administrative tool when planning or delivering induction. For example, if a presentation is being arranged the organizer will need to remember the following points:

- book room
- check equipment
- arrange catering
- send details to participants
- confirm arrangements with speaker

The induction manager could make similar lists available to everyone involved in delivering training as a means of ensuring a consistent approach. The use of standard checklists can help to save time and prevent disasters caused by bad planning. The one thing that can be guaranteed to stick in the mind of the participants is the part that goes wrong. Using a checklist will make it less likely that the coffee will fail to turn up or that the guest speaker has to mime because the video recorder has gone missing.

5.1.3 | *Induction packs*

In some libraries newcomers are given an induction pack containing basic information, to which they can add other material as necessary. Depending on resources, this may range from a simple cardboard folder to a stylish wallet. Whatever is used, it is a good idea to personalize the pack, perhaps by printing the individual's name on the front. Seeing that some effort has been spent on their behalf will almost certainly be appreciated by any new staff member. An induction pack, including first day reporting instructions and a timetable, may be sent to the new recruit before they start work. This has the advantage of making the person feel welcome even before they arrive and of allowing them to digest the information at their own pace. On the other hand, the first day is also a good opportunity to present the induction pack in person, allowing any questions to be dealt with immediately. In addition, the possibility is avoided of the new recruit forgetting to bring their induction pack to work and replacement copies of everything having to be found. The initial contents of an induction pack might include the following:

- a staffing chart
- a plan of the layout of the library
- checklist covering the first two or three weeks
- information about the parent organization
- guide to library services

- procedures for reporting sick, taking leave etc.
- additional material such as bus timetables, local map etc.

5.2 Evaluation

There are two principal reasons for evaluating training. Firstly, to analyse the benefits resulting from the investment of resources and, secondly, to assess the effectiveness with which stated aims and objectives have been met. In measuring effectiveness, both the success of the induction programme itself and the achievements of the individual should be assessed. The way in which the programme evolves and develops over time should be in response to weaknesses or problems identified during the evaluative stage of the cycle. The gathering of evaluative information should be ongoing and a variety of methods may be employed.

5.2.1 *Analysing benefits*

Techniques such as cost-benefit analysis have been developed to evaluate training in monetary terms, emphasizing the financial measurement of everything, including human behaviour. Whereas such methods can be very powerful tools for justifying investment in training, they do require a level of expertise which is beyond many library services. Indeed, the amount of effort required may seem disproportionate to the usefulness of the end results. Induction poses particular problems for this type of evaluation because training and job performance tend to blur into one another to such an extent that it is virtually impossible to identify where one ends and the other begins.

5.2.2 *Evaluating the induction programme*

The purpose of evaluating is to consider how successful the programme was in achieving the objectives that were established at the outset. For instance, one of the objectives might have stated that, 'by the end of the induction programme each member of staff will understand the layout of the library and the immediate environment'. As long as the selected method results in new staff being able to find their way around, the objective will have been met and there will be no need to adjust that aspect of the programme. If it is demonstrated that significant numbers of new staff have real problems in becoming familiar with the layout it may be necessary to rethink the way in which they are shown round. Often, it may be necessary to make some slight adjustments on the basis of evaluative information but, even if no changes are necessary, it is still important to evaluate on each occasion to ensure that the method and content continue to be appropriate. At the same time, it should be remembered that everyone has different perceptions and different learning needs. Care should be taken to avoid making constant changes to a basically sound programme in response to the comments of individuals who may not necessarily be representative of all new staff.

Various methods of assessing the programme may be used. Verbal feedback may be sought from participants during regular review sessions and after the induction period has finished. It is useful to structure such discussions to ensure that all aspects are covered, rather than asking in a general way if everything is all right. Evaluation forms or 'happiness sheets' may be used at the end of a course or after a particular event, such as a visit or group training exercise. They are useful for providing an instant response but do have limitations. For example, people are often anxious to leave at the end of a session and do not want to spend time writing down what they thought about the trainer or the accommodation. They may feel more inclined to tick boxes on a very simple form but the level of information provided only allows for a superficial assessment. One solution is to combine frequent and brief verbal feedback with a more comprehensive written evaluation which is completed after the induction period has finished. This enables individuals to comment on the programme as it is happening, directly to their supervisor or manager. Then later, they are able to take a longer view of the programme in its entirety and make a more considered assessment of its merits and weaknesses. Aspects which should be covered include pace, content, relevance, level of detail and style of delivery, among others.

5.2.3   *Assessing individual progress*

Most library induction programmes place a great deal more emphasis on input than outcomes. In other words, they concentrate on what people are going to receive in the way of training and information rather than on how the training will be put into practice in a work situation. After all, there is a positive sense of achievement to be gained for both the provider and the recipient of induction packs, courses and training sessions. Conversely, the very thought of testing the resulting skills or knowledge can have negative connotations for many people, perhaps reminding them of school exams or driving tests. The fact that outcomes are so difficult to measure, especially where the emphasis is on qualitative rather than quantitative assessment, is not helpful. In addition, testing may seem inappropriate whilst new skills, knowledge and attitudes are still in the process of being acquired.

However, it is still necessary to find out whether learning outcomes or objectives are actually being achieved. The induction manager may select from a range of techniques including observation, questionnaires, log books and interviews. These methods are all well documented but none is without drawbacks, particularly when assessing a service rather than, say, a manufacturing industry. In deciding which are most the appropriate means, the abilities of the staff who will conduct the assessment must be considered. Supervisors and managers may need training themselves to ensure that they not only know how to perform the testing but also are able to interpret and act on the results. Obviously, it is preferable that assessment should be conducted in an atmosphere of trust. The whole experience is likely to be much more positive if the new recruit fully understands the reasons for assessment and is a willing participant. From the start, it should be stressed that the overriding concern is for the quality of service provided to users. When viewed in those terms the emphasis is shifted from individual performance as an end in itself to the contribution that each person is expected to make to their team, the library service and the parent organization.

5.2.4   *Feedback*

There must be opportunities throughout the induction programme for new staff to receive and give feedback. Ideally, progress reviews should take place at regular intervals with a final session scheduled at the end of the induction period. The usual process would be for the supervisor to spend some time with the new recruit, perhaps weekly, discussing how all aspects of the programme are going. The aim should be to retain motivation while being realistic about progress. Therefore praise should be given for real achievements but any problems must also be raised and discussed. The individual must be given the opportunity to comment on how they view their own achievements and whether they feel that particular circumstances are affecting their progress. It is important, at this stage, to identify any weaknesses and take steps to rectify them. Small problems may grow into much larger ones if they are not tackled at an early stage. The final session may usefully be conducted by a more senior member of staff, perhaps the induction manager if this is feasible. This meeting also provides the opportunity for seeking feedback from the individual about the induction programme itself.

5.2.5 Completing the cycle

As already suggested, evaluation should be an ongoing process, rather than a sudden event at the end of induction. However, the end of the programme is an appropriate point to bring together all of the threads. This is the time to consider the strengths and weaknesses of the programme and decide what adjustments may be necessary before the next recruits arrive. By responding to careful evaluation, induction can be a dynamic process, constantly evolving to meet the changing needs of the organization and the new staff joining it.

5.3 Summary

- Induction should not be optional. Failure to provide staff induction can result in long-term problems for both employers and employees.
- All newly recruited, promoted or transferred staff need an induction programme which takes account of their particular circumstances.
- A systematic approach is the most effective. Aims and objectives should be clarified before attempting to devise ways of delivering the programme. The ongoing cycle must include evaluation.
- Attention must be paid to detail. For example, providing a personalized folder and a clean desk can help to establish a productive and harmonious working relationship from the start.
- There are many ways of providing induction. Using a variety of approaches will stimulate interest and help to satisfy the different learning needs of individuals.
- Communication, as always, is of paramount importance. Regular opportunities for feedback and discussion should form an integral part of the programme.
- Good intentions are not enough. Someone, such as an induction manager, has to make sure that the theory is translated into sound practice. All those involved must possess the skills and knowledge necessary to deliver a carefully planned and designed induction programme.

Selective bibliography

Advisory Conciliation and Arbitration Service, *Induction of new employees*, London, ACAS, 1991, (Advisory booklet number 7).

Blanksby, M., *Staff training: a librarian's handbook*, Newcastle under Lyme, Association of Assistant Librarians, 1988.

Buckley, R. and Caple, J., *The theory and practice of training*, 2nd edn., London, Kogan Page, 1992.

Clutterbuck, D., *Everyone needs a mentor: fostering talent at work*, 2nd edn., London, Institute of Personnel Management, 1991.

Corder, C., *Teaching hard, teaching soft*, Aldershot, Gower, 1990.

Fowler, A., *A good start: effective employee induction*, 2nd edn., London, Institute of Personnel Management, 1990.

Jones, N. and Jordan, P., *Staff management in library and information work*, 2nd edn., Aldershot, Gower, 1987.

Kirby, J., *Induction training for non-professional library staff: a basic programme*, Sheffield City Polytechnic, 1984.

Meighan, M., *How to design and deliver induction training programmes*, London, Kogan Page, 1991.

Phillips, J., *Handbook of training evaluation and measurement methods*, 2nd edn., London, Kogan Page, 1991.

Prytherch, R. (ed.), *Handbook of library training practice*, Aldershot, Gower, 1986.

Rae, L., *How to measure training effectiveness*, 2nd edn., Aldershot, Gower, 1991.

Skeats, J., *Successful induction: how to get the most from your new employees*, London, Kogan Page, 1991.

Watts-Davies, R., *Induction*, 3rd edn., London, Industrial Society, 1989, (Notes for managers).

Williams, T., *Effective debriefing: the key to learning*, London, BACIE, 1991.

Videos

For starters, Melrose Film Productions, 26 mins.

The induction tapes: strategies for new staff, Longman Training, 1990, 48 mins.

Right from day one: getting the most from new employees, Longman Training, 1987, 10 mins.

Useful addresses

The following organizations have expertise in the field of induction training. As well as maintaining collections in their own libraries they also publish material on, or relevant to, staff induction.

ACAS (Advisory, Conciliation and Arbitration Service)
Head Office
27 Wilton Street
London SW1X 7AZ

British Association for Commercial and Industrial Education (BACIE)
16 Park Crescent
London W1N 4AP

The Industrial Society
Peter Runge House
3 Carlton House Terrace
London SW1Y 5DG

The Institute of Management
Management House
Cottingham Road
Corby
Northants NN17 1TT

Institute of Personnel Management
IPM House
35 Camp Road
Wimbledon
London SW19 4UX

The Library Association
7 Ridgmount Street
London WC1E 7AE

Examples

*1. *Induction programmes: Statement of Objectives*
   (County of Avon – Community Leisure Department)

*2. Aims and objectives for the *INTRODUCTION TO A.L.I.S.*
   PROGRAMME
   (County of Avon – Community Leisure Department)

 3. Library Assistant's induction checklist
   (University of the West of England, Bristol)

*4. *SAMPLE INDUCTION CHECKLIST*
   (for use by Supervisors)
   (County of Avon – Community Leisure Department, BRISTOL
    SOUTH)

 5. Sample induction sessions
   (Thames Valley University)

 6. Mentoring
   (Middlesex University)

 7. Feedback to the new member of staff
   (Manchester Metropolitan University)

*8. *EVALUATION FORMS*
   (County of Avon – Community Leisure Department)

Thanks are due to the organizations named above for allowing extracts from their induction programmes to be reproduced.

* Taken from an *INDUCTION HANDBOOK* for Managers and
   Supervisors. Price £5. Available from: May Curtis
                                           Staff Development Officer
                                           Community Leisure Department
                                           Avonquay Resource Centre
                                           Cumberland Basin
                                           Bristol BS1 6XL

Example 1

4.	THE INDUCTION PROGRAMME

A. What will be achieved?

By the end of the Induction Programme a newcomer will:

* be clear about the scope of the job and what is expected of her/him - both by the manager and the Department.

* have a full understanding of the conditions of service which govern the appointment - and all related procedures (eg. grievance procedures)

* be familiar with the physical and social environment of the job.

* know about local customs and rules.

* be familiar with County Policies and Procedures which govern service delivery and employment eg. Health & Safety, Equal Opportunities.

* feel welcome by the organisation at a local, area, departmental, county level.

* be familiar with all Department/County Systems/procedures relevant to the job function eg. Administration/Finance/Communication/Computer.

* be aware of the wider context ie. the Area/Department/County structure within which the job will be done.

* be familiar with the Philosophy/Mission of the Department and the Aims and Objectives of the service/area/section that s/he has joined.

So that:

All immediate anxieties are allayed and the newcomer is able to settle to learning the job from a sound information base.

5

Example 2

AIMS & OBJECTIVES

AIMS

- To introduce new staff to the wider AVON LIBRARY & INFORMATION SERVICE of which they are part.

- To promote a sense of belonging to a wider service.

- To provide an opportunity to make contact with staff from other Libraries/Departments.

- To meet staff involved in Specialist/Support Services.

- To enable staff to offer a better service to the public

OBJECTIVES

At the end of the course participants will be able to:

* List the Support Services that operate from College Green and describe what each service does.

* Describe briefly the Specialist Services on offer to the Public in the Central Library.

* Explain the role and work of the Librarian for Special Groups and the Library Services Development Officers.

* Describe the role and work of the School Library Service.

* Describe the work of the Bindery.

* Say what are the significant differences between Automated and Non-automated sites.

* Describe a day in the life of a Mobile.

* Appreciate the impact of the County Services on the Work of their branch/department.

* Identify the commonalities in their work and some of the varieties that exist by exchanging experiences with other participants.

* Appreciate their position in the wider organisation in which they work. (i.e. ALIS)

Example 3

LIBRARY ASSISTANTS INDUCTION CHECKLIST

YOUR FIRST DAY

WELCOME TO BOLLAND!

I.   INTRODUCTIONS

       Your Office
           Your desk
           Locker and key
           Staff notice boards and rotas
           Security Issues
           Stationery supplies

       Your Team and Office Mates
           Manager
           Supervisor
           Team members
           Other office mates
           Mentor

       Other facilities
           Staff entrance to the library
           Toilets
           Staff room

II.   THE WORKING DAY

       The induction pack & programme

       Parking permits
       Hours of work; lunch hours and tea breaks
       Standards of dress
       Annual leave & Time in Lieu
       Pay
       Telephone calls
       What you should do if....
       Policies and procedures manuals

       Where you fit in: the role of a Library Assistant
           Shelf tidying & shelving
           Issue Desks
           Team responsibilities or specific duties of the post:
           _____

III.   TOUR OF THE SITE

       Car & bike parking
       Buses & bus stops
       Felixstowe Court restaurant and bar
       The refectory
       Shops, bank, & laundrette
       Recreational facilities
       The Octagon & Chaplaincy   PTO

Example 3 continued

YOUR FIRST WEEK

IV.   JOB TRAINING

Shelf Tidying & Shelving
            The rota & tidying times
            The Dewey system
            Trolleys
            Tables and "dump" trolleys
            Quality control

Team jobs:-

_____

_____

_____

Operating library equipment
            Photocopiers
            Microform equipment
            AV equipment
            Binding & laminating equipment

Begin Issue Desk Training -- *Please see separate checklist*

V.   HEALTH AND SAFETY MATTERS

Personal responsibility:-
            Sickness forms
            Moving heavy objects
            Using VDU's
            No smoking rules
            Keeping gangways & exits clear of obstruction (& general tidiness)
            Closing the fire doors
            Accident reporting
            Hazard report forms
            Reporting to supervisors after 6.00 pm
            Policy PD11 & Bolland Safety Manual (where they are)

In an emergency:-
            When an alarm sounds
            Action of discovering a fire

Tour and demonstration:
            Fire alarm points
            Fire exits
            Assembly point after evacuation
            Location of fire equipment
            How to use the fire equipment
            The first aid box & first aiders list

Example 3 continued

VI.   <u>TOUR OF THE LIBRARY & INTRODUCTIONS TO LIBRARY STAFF</u>

2 staircases + lift.
On all floors: "OPACS" and photocopiers;

<u>Level 2</u>

Resources: The issue desk & short loan
                          Current periodicals & newspapers

People: Acquisitions and periodicals team
                          Inter-library loans team
                          Circulations team

<u>Level 3</u>

Resources &   Back issues of periodicals
Facilities: The Reference Area
                          Abstracts and Indexes
                          CD-ROM and online databases
                          The main Enquiry Desk
                          Statistics
                          Women's Toilets

People: The B.E.S.T. Team

<u>Level 4</u>

Resources &
Facilities: Books: class numbers 001-499
                          The Law section
                          Official publications
                          The AV Area
                          Men's Toilets

People: Subject Librarians

<u>Level 5</u>

Resources &
Facilities: Books: class numbers 500-999
                          Women's Toilets
                          Teaching Room 5D10
                          5D9 - Room for Academic staff & photocopier

People: Subject Librarians
                          The TOP Team
                          The Library Management Team (LMT)
                          The IT Librarian and Assistant
                          Val, LMT's secretary   PTO

Example 3 continued

<u>YOUR FIRST MONTH</u>

VII.   <u>AN OVERVIEW OF THE BOLLAND LIBRARY</u>

<u>What the library does</u>:
　　　　　Customer care and what it means
　　　　　Working with the faculties: selecting resources and teaching
　　　　　Acquiring new materials (books, periodicals, indexes, AV and IT)
　　　　　Cataloguing & accessions lists
　　　　　Processing & shelving
　　　　　Lending
　　　　　Reference and Enquiries

<u>Staff structure: who does what</u>
　　　　　The Management Team & Central staff
　　　　　The Site Librarian
　　　　　Subject Librarians
　　　　　Academic Services Teams
　　　　　User Services Teams

VIII. <u>THE LIBRARY IN CONTEXT</u>

The University
Objectives and Policies of the Library
Cross-site structure and channels of communication

The University Induction Programme

IX.   <u>CONTINUING TRAINING AND DEVELOPMENT</u>

Induction follow-up
Further training opportunities
Procedure for attending training events
Courses from the Computer Centre (eg, WordPerfect)
Membership of the Library Association

Example 3 continued

AND LATER....

WHO'S WHO AND WHAT THEY DO

The Library Management Team
The IT Librarian and Assistant
The Site Librarian
Subject Librarians
Academic Services teams
The Acquisitions team
The Periodicals Team
The Technical Services Team
The Circulations Team
Inter-library Loans
Special Services:
Special Services Librarian
Advisor to Part-time Students
Audiovisual team

GETTING THE BEST OUT OF LIBERTAS

SITE VISITS

Bower Ashton
Redland
St. Matthias

Example 4

SAMPLE FOR AN AREA

INDUCTION CHECKLIST (for use by Supervisor)

NAME...

STARDATE...

ACTION	DATE	WHOSE RE-SPONSIBILITY	WHEN COMPLETED
Before starting: 1. Induction pack sent. 2. Statement of terms and conditions. 3. Induction programme drawings. 4. Note to staff of his/her arrival.			
Reception New employee to be received by:			
Introduction to organisation 1. Tea/coffee arrangements 2. Lunchtime arrangements 3. Personal 'phone calls. 4. Expenses			
Building 1. Toilets 2. Kitchen 3. Fire exits/exting-uishers/alarms. 4. Tour and intro-duction to other staff. 5. Keys.			

Example 4 continued

ACTION	DATE	WHOSE RESPONSIBILITY	WHEN COMPLETED
Structure of Department 1. Management structure. 2. Role of Department. 3. Roles of different parts of department. 4. Check receipt of induction pack.			
Work of new employee's part of department. 1. Roles of individuals within the department. 2. Role of new employee.			
Conditions of employment. a) **Pay** 1. Bank details to 2. P45 to 3. Explain how and when paid. 4. Check receipt of conditions of employment etc. b) **Hours/Sickness/Holiday** 1. Hours of work 2. Sickness procedure. 3. Issue leave sheet & procedure for booking and current entitlement. c) **Health and Safety** 1. Check receipt of Health and Safety guidelines. 2. Introduce First Aider. 3. Explain Safety Officer's role. 4. Accident book. 5. First Aid box. 6. Fire Drill. 7. Use of extinguishers. d) **Trade Union** 1. Introduce to rep/pass on contact. e) **Grievance/disciplinary procedure** 1. Check receipt of guidelines.			

Example 4 continued

ACTION	DATE	WHOSE RESPONSIBILITY	WHEN COMPLETED
Job Needs a) **Machines - how/where** 1. Photocopier. 2. Telephone/how to answer/ useful numbers. 3. Typewriter. 4. Computer. 5. Security alarm. b) **Correspondence** 1. Stationery 2. Addresses 3. Internal mailing systems 4. Stamps c) **Diary.**			

Example 5

Induction Session A2

GENERAL INTRODUCTION TO THE INSTITUTION AND SERVICE

Head of Library and Information Services

<u>Objectives</u>:

At the end of this session the new member of staff will have an understanding and appreciation of the structure and mission of TVU and its Library and Information Service.

<u>Main areas to be covered</u>:

Institutional structure:

      Directorate
      Schools
      Sites

Students and courses:

      Types of course
      Modes of attendance
      Ethnic mix

Future of the institution:

      Teaching and learning
      Teaching and learning resource centres
      Physical developments

Library and Information Services:

      Staffing structure
      Physical accommodation
      Service strategies (student-driven!)
      Future developments
      Communication/decision making: meetings, staff bulletins
      Membership and access policy
      Role of Head of Library and Information Services

<u>Training materials and supporting documentation to be used</u> (videos, handouts, procedure instructions, policy documents etc):

      Directory of LIS staff and sites
      List of Schools

<u>Other notes</u> (eg duration of typical session):

      1 hour

Example 5 | continued

Induction Session B7

THE ENQUIRY SERVICE

Site Services Librarian or delegate

Objectives:

At the end of this session the new member of staff:

a.   will be able to locate information at the Enquiry Desk

b.   will understand the role and function of Enquiry Desk service

Main areas to be covered:

The role of the Enquiry Desk as a permanently staffed first port of call for users with information needs queries.

The timetabling of the Enquiry Desk

The arrangement and layout of the Desk: stationery

The Enquiry Desk manual

The possible range of enquiries including telephone enquiries

Telephone, use of

The use of Quick Reference materials: statistics, etc.

Database enquiries: cover and prioritisation

Inter-personal relations and the decoding of enquiries

Sharing the load: when to call on colleagues for help

Access and visitors book including access policy, franchised students, London Plus

Enrolment of students (at Slough)

Other stationery eg notices, manuals for photocopiers

Training materials and supporting documentation to be used (videos, handouts, procedure instructions, policy documents etc):

As above, eg Enquiry Desk manual
            Enrolment/Circo manual
            Visitors manual

Other notes (eg duration of typical session):

1 hour for Enquiry Desk staff

Example 5 continued

Induction Session C4

PERIODICALS DEPARTMENT

Senior Library Assistant - Periodicals

Objectives:

The new member of staff will:

-   Have an overall understanding of the work of the Periodicals
    Department and how it interfaces with other library areas.

-   Be able to deal with basic queries relating to periodicals, and know
    which staff members to refer more complex ones to.

Main areas to be covered:

Introductions to Periodicals staff

The size and coverage of the Periodicals collection

General introduction to the basic routines of the department, to be
covered in greater detail in the course of the induction tour:
    Ordering (new subscriptions and renewals)
    Payment
    Receipt
    Stock recording
    Display
    Maintenance of displayed stock
    Sorting and distribution of mail

Interconnections and relations with other departments;
    Acquisitions; Subject Librarians; Cataloguing

Stock records - purpose and methods:
    Periodical entries on OPAC
    BLCMP Subs. Control (payment)
    Kardex (receipt and claims)
    Index cards

Layout of the open access collection:
    The main alphabetical sequence
    Other sequences: newspapers; abstracts and indexes; restricted
    access collection: Quick Reference; microfilm; agendas and minutes
    of institutional meetings
    Stock maintenance: weeding; tidying; security

Current priorities and future plans

Training materials and supporting documentation to be used (videos,
handouts, procedure instructions, policy documents etc):

-   examples of relevant stationery and documentation will be used
    during the course of the induction (LRF, Serials Amendment Form,
    agents' renewal lists, invoices etc)

-   trainee will be shown the location of the Periodicals Information
    Book and staff manual.

Other notes (eg duration of typical session):

Typical session will last about 1 hour but could be longer, depending
onthe specialist intersts of the trainee.

Example 6

Paper MT/92/92

MIDDLESEX UNIVERSITY

HUMAN RESOURCES POLICY STATEMENT HR2

<u>Mentoring</u>

Middlesex University recognises the special needs of all staff when they are first employed by the University. To meet these needs in addition to the provision of introduction, induction and specific staff development programmes (the latter on an on-going basis - see Human Resources Policy Statement HR1) the University will provide each new member of staff with a mentor during his/her first year of employment.

Mentoring is essentially the assignment of a new member of staff (mentee) to the relatively informal tutelage of a more experience colleague (mentor). In most cases, it would be expected that the mentor and mentee would share the same discipline or experiential background; but there may well be circumstances when other considerations or factors take precedence. What matters is that the mentor is recognised for the quality of, for instance, teaching, their general knowledge of the working of the University, and their personal qualities that are likely to make them sympathetic to the development needs of the mentee (in this latter context, someone with recent experience as a mentee may well have something to offer). It is <u>not</u> desirable that the mentor should be in a line management role of the mentee, nor that he/she will have any involvement in formal assessment of the mentee with regard to, for example, satisfactory completion of a probationary period.

The mentor's role is to establish a working relationship of trust and support with the mentee, and thereby to offer advice, assistance and direction (as appropriate) with a view to promoting the mentee's performance and competence in their new post. This may well involve discussion to identify what the mentee needs to know and learn, and what skills he/she needs to develop or refine; it could also involve, in the case of teaching staff, mentor and mentee visiting each other's classes and, in the case of other staff, workbase visits as the basis for further discussion on themes related to good classroom practice; and it is likely to involve the mentor in helping the mentee map out a programme for personal and professional development in the institution - a "learning plan". At this stage, the mentor is likely to be of value in helping the mentee chart his/her progress and achievement, and in compiling a portfolio of materials whereby to demonstrate this achievement.

The mentor role is important, therefore, not only for the mentee but also for the promotion of a quality culture; additionally, it can serve as a form of on-going staff development for the mentor him/herself.

Example 6 continued

- 2 -

The University recognises that the desirable qualities in a mentor include: ready availability and approachability; a willingness to listen; and an ability to be sympathetic and alert to the challenges facing a new member of staff. For a mentor to valuably carry out the role, he/she is likely to give some significant time to the needs of the mentee. The University expects that this contribution to staff development will be recognised as an element in the mentor's overall work programme.

This policy was adopted by Management Team at its meeting on

KHG/SEF
9 November 1992

[papers nr2.pol]

Example 7

FEEDBACK TO THE NEW MEMBER OF STAFF

Everyone joining is keen to know how they are progressing in their work and is fitting into the department/section.

The initial period of employment either with a new employer or in a significantly different job is important and it is essential that staff receive proper support and guidance.

In the University we have a probationary period for support staff of 13 weeks but what is contained here is outside the context of that process.

It is strongly recommended that the head of department or immediate supervisor meet with the new colleague at regular intervals in order to discuss progress. A meeting every two weeks is suggested.

The head or supervisor should seek the answers to the following questions:-

* Which part of your job have you enjoyed?

* Which part of your job have you found most difficult?

* How do you think you have 'fitted in' to the department?

* What aspect of your job do you feel you need assistance with?

* How do you feel about the way you have been inducted into the department?

Ensure that the space you book to meet in is quiet and you are not likely to be interrupted.

Make notes, but state clearly you are not preparing a report but to ensure that you remember to take action where necessary.

Give time for the person to speak, put them at thier ease, allow sufficient time for the meeting.

Gather information from colleagues so that you can:-

a)   Praise for work performed well;

b)   Give feedback on what can be improved.

Ind.Tr.Gui.Plan 11.92.

32

Example 8

COMMUNITY LEISURE INDUCTION

EVALUATION FORM (1)

NAME OF NEWCOMER/INDUCTEE......................................

NAME OF RESPONSIBLE MANAGER ....

Location/Office ....

Start Date ....

Please complete this after 3 months.

Please tick where appropriate and add comment where necesary.

A. ORGANISATION   COMMENTS

1. Did you receive your programme

   before start date   ☐
   on start date   ☐
   after start date   ☐?

2. Before you started were you clear about
   what would be happening on your first day?

   very   ☐
   vaguely   ☐
   not at all   ☐

3. To what extent did the programme planner
   contribute to the effectiveness of the
   Induction Programme.

   considerably ☐
   moderately   ☐
   not at all   ☐

4. Were your new colleagues/contacts prepared
   to greet/meet you.

   yes - all   ☐
   yes - some   ☐
   not at all   ☐

5. Were you involved in reviewing and amending
   the Induction Programme where appropriate.

   yes ☐   no ☐

Example 8 continued

COMMUNITY LEISURE INDUCTION

<u>EVALUATION FORM (1) (continued)</u>   <u>COMMENTS</u>

<u>B. THE PACK</u>

1. Was the information given in the INDUCTION
   PACK useful i.e. relevant, clear, timely,
   sufficient. Please write comments.

2. What was missing?

3. Were you given the opportunity to clarify
   understanding/ask questions about the
   Information?

   Yes ☐   No ☐

<u>C THE PROGRAMME</u>

Please refer to the Objectives for induction
in your Pack.

1. Please indicate to what extent the objectives
   have been achieved so far for you through the
   <u>planned programme</u>.

   1.   ☐ fully   ☐ partially   ☐ not at all.

   2.   ☐   ☐   ☐

   3.   ☐   ☐   ☐

   4.   ☐   ☐   ☐

   5.   ☐   ☐   ☐

   6.   ☐   ☐   ☐

   7.   ☐   ☐   ☐

   8.   ☐   ☐   ☐

   9.   ☐   ☐   ☐

   10. ☐   ☐   ☐

Example 8 continued

COMMUNITY LEISURE INDUCTION
EVALUATION FORM (1) (continued. 2)   COMMENTS

2. Have objectives been achieved other than through the
   programme programme? If so please describe how:

3. How have you been able to contribute to achieving
   the objectives?

4. What still needs to happen?

5. Have you had the opportunity to discuss your
   immediate training needs with your line
   manager following Induction.

   Yes ☐   No ☐

FURTHER COMMENTS

Please sign and post to The Staff Development and Training Officer, Avonquay Resource
Centre, Cumberland Basin, Bristol   BS1 6XL.

Signed_____   Date_____

ACLO/County Officer Signature _____

Example 8 continued

COMMUNITY LEISURE INDUCTION

<u>EVALUATION FORM (2)</u>

Responsible Manager _____

Newcomer/Inductee _____

Please record <u>briefly</u> the principle successes and difficulties relating to the above employee's Induction. It is suggested that a copy be retained by you to assist in completing the more detailed Annual Survey.

1. <u>PLANNING/PREPARATION BEFORE 1ST DAY</u>

   <u>ORGANISATION:</u>

   <u>CONTENT/OBJECTIVES:</u>

   <u>OTHER</u>

2. <u>DURING THE PROGRAMME</u>

   <u>ORGANISATION:</u>

   <u>CONTENT/OBJECTIVES:</u>

   <u>OTHER</u>

Signed _____   Date _____

ACLO/County Officer Signature _____

Index